50 Low-Fat Dinners for Home

By: Kelly Johnson

Table of Contents

- Grilled Chicken with Quinoa Salad
- Baked Salmon with Steamed Vegetables
- Zucchini Noodles with Pesto
- Turkey and Veggie Stir-Fry
- Roasted Chicken with Sweet Potatoes
- Shrimp and Broccoli Stir-Fry
- Veggie Tacos with Black Beans
- Grilled Tilapia with Brown Rice
- Spaghetti Squash with Marinara Sauce
- Baked Cod with Asparagus
- Cauliflower Rice Stir-Fry
- Chicken and Vegetable Skewers
- Baked Turkey Meatballs with Zoodles
- Lentil and Vegetable Soup
- Spicy Baked Tofu with Steamed Greens
- Stuffed Bell Peppers with Ground Turkey
- Grilled Chicken Caesar Salad (light dressing)
- Black Bean and Quinoa Salad
- Salmon with Roasted Brussels Sprouts
- Chicken Lettuce Wraps
- Veggie and Chickpea Curry
- Baked Chicken Parmesan with Zucchini Noodles
- Grilled Veggie Skewers
- Eggplant Stir-Fry with Tofu
- Shrimp and Avocado Salad
- Roasted Sweet Potato with Black Beans
- Chicken Fajitas with Bell Peppers
- Roasted Salmon with Cucumber and Tomato Salad
- Lemon Garlic Grilled Shrimp
- Chickpea and Spinach Stew
- Roasted Cauliflower with Tahini Dressing
- Grilled Portobello Mushrooms with Quinoa
- Sautéed Spinach and Garlic Chicken
- Veggie-Packed Whole Wheat Pasta
- Grilled Chicken and Cucumber Salad

- Spicy Grilled Shrimp with Avocado Salsa
- Quinoa-Stuffed Tomatoes
- Light Turkey Chili
- Grilled Eggplant and Tomato Stack
- Spaghetti Squash with Garlic and Herbs
- Shrimp Scampi with Zucchini Noodles
- Grilled Turkey Burgers with Sweet Potato Fries
- Quinoa and Black Bean Lettuce Wraps
- Roasted Veggie Buddha Bowl
- Baked Chicken with Roasted Veggies
- Tofu Stir-Fry with Brown Rice
- Spaghetti with Tomato Basil Sauce
- Grilled Chicken with Mango Salsa
- Sweet Potato and Kale Salad
- Grilled Shrimp Tacos with Slaw

Grilled Chicken with Quinoa Salad

Ingredients:

- 2 boneless, skinless chicken breasts
- 1 tablespoon olive oil
- Salt and pepper to taste
- 1 cup quinoa
- 2 cups water or vegetable broth
- 1 cucumber, diced
- 1/2 cup cherry tomatoes, halved
- 1/4 cup red onion, diced
- 1 tablespoon fresh parsley, chopped
- Juice of 1 lemon
- 2 tablespoons olive oil (for salad dressing)
- Salt and pepper to taste

Instructions:

1. Preheat the grill to medium-high heat. Season chicken breasts with olive oil, salt, and pepper.
2. Grill chicken for 6-8 minutes per side until fully cooked and the internal temperature reaches 165°F (74°C).
3. While the chicken is grilling, rinse quinoa under cold water and cook it according to package instructions using water or vegetable broth.
4. In a bowl, combine the cooked quinoa, cucumber, cherry tomatoes, red onion, and parsley.
5. Drizzle with lemon juice, olive oil, salt, and pepper, and toss to combine.
6. Serve the grilled chicken on top of the quinoa salad. Enjoy!

Baked Salmon with Steamed Vegetables

Ingredients:

- 2 salmon fillets
- 1 tablespoon olive oil
- 1 teaspoon garlic powder
- 1 teaspoon dried thyme
- Salt and pepper to taste
- 1 cup broccoli florets
- 1 cup carrots, sliced
- 1 tablespoon butter

Instructions:

1. Preheat the oven to 400°F (200°C). Line a baking sheet with parchment paper and place the salmon fillets on it.
2. Drizzle the salmon with olive oil and season with garlic powder, thyme, salt, and pepper.
3. Bake for 12-15 minutes until the salmon is cooked through and flakes easily with a fork.
4. Steam the broccoli and carrots until tender (about 5-7 minutes). Toss the vegetables with butter.
5. Serve the baked salmon alongside the steamed vegetables. Enjoy!

Zucchini Noodles with Pesto

Ingredients:

- 3 medium zucchinis, spiralized into noodles
- 1 cup fresh basil leaves
- 1/4 cup pine nuts
- 2 garlic cloves
- 1/4 cup grated Parmesan cheese
- 1/4 cup olive oil
- Salt and pepper to taste

Instructions:

1. In a food processor, combine basil, pine nuts, garlic, Parmesan, olive oil, salt, and pepper. Pulse until smooth to make the pesto.
2. In a skillet, sauté zucchini noodles over medium heat for 2-3 minutes until tender.
3. Toss the zucchini noodles with the pesto sauce until evenly coated.
4. Serve immediately as a light and flavorful meal.

Turkey and Veggie Stir-Fry

Ingredients:

- 1 lb ground turkey
- 2 tablespoons olive oil
- 1 red bell pepper, sliced
- 1 zucchini, sliced
- 1/2 cup snap peas
- 2 garlic cloves, minced
- 2 tablespoons soy sauce
- 1 tablespoon honey
- 1 teaspoon sesame oil
- 1 tablespoon sesame seeds (optional)

Instructions:

1. Heat olive oil in a large skillet over medium heat. Add the ground turkey and cook until browned, breaking it up as it cooks.
2. Add the bell pepper, zucchini, and snap peas to the skillet. Sauté for 5-7 minutes until the vegetables are tender.
3. Add garlic and cook for an additional minute.
4. Stir in soy sauce, honey, and sesame oil. Cook for 1-2 minutes until the sauce thickens slightly.
5. Garnish with sesame seeds (optional) and serve immediately.

Roasted Chicken with Sweet Potatoes

Ingredients:

- 2 bone-in, skin-on chicken thighs
- 2 medium sweet potatoes, cubed
- 2 tablespoons olive oil
- 1 teaspoon paprika
- 1 teaspoon garlic powder
- Salt and pepper to taste
- Fresh rosemary sprigs (optional)

Instructions:

1. Preheat the oven to 400°F (200°C). Place chicken thighs and sweet potatoes on a baking sheet.
2. Drizzle with olive oil, then season the chicken and sweet potatoes with paprika, garlic powder, salt, and pepper.
3. Roast for 30-35 minutes, flipping the sweet potatoes halfway through, until the chicken reaches an internal temperature of 165°F (74°C) and the sweet potatoes are tender.
4. Serve the roasted chicken with the sweet potatoes. Enjoy!

Shrimp and Broccoli Stir-Fry

Ingredients:

- 1 lb shrimp, peeled and deveined
- 2 tablespoons olive oil
- 2 cups broccoli florets
- 1 red bell pepper, sliced
- 2 garlic cloves, minced
- 1/4 cup soy sauce
- 1 tablespoon honey
- 1 tablespoon sesame oil
- 1 teaspoon grated ginger

Instructions:

1. Heat olive oil in a large skillet over medium heat. Add shrimp and cook for 2-3 minutes per side until pink. Remove and set aside.
2. In the same skillet, add broccoli and bell pepper. Cook for 5-7 minutes until the vegetables are tender.
3. Add garlic and ginger and cook for another 1-2 minutes.
4. Stir in soy sauce, honey, and sesame oil. Add shrimp back into the skillet and toss everything together.
5. Serve immediately with steamed rice or on its own.

Veggie Tacos with Black Beans

Ingredients:

- 1 can black beans, drained and rinsed
- 1 tablespoon olive oil
- 1/2 onion, chopped
- 1 zucchini, diced
- 1 red bell pepper, diced
- 1/2 teaspoon cumin
- 1/2 teaspoon chili powder
- Salt and pepper to taste
- 8 small corn tortillas
- Fresh cilantro, chopped
- Salsa for topping

Instructions:

1. Heat olive oil in a skillet over medium heat. Add the onion and cook for 2-3 minutes until softened.
2. Add zucchini and bell pepper and cook for another 5-7 minutes until tender.
3. Stir in black beans, cumin, chili powder, salt, and pepper. Cook for 2-3 minutes until heated through.
4. Warm the tortillas in a pan or microwave. Fill each tortilla with the veggie and black bean mixture.
5. Top with fresh cilantro and salsa. Serve immediately.

Grilled Tilapia with Brown Rice

Ingredients:

- 2 tilapia fillets
- 1 tablespoon olive oil
- 1 teaspoon paprika
- 1 teaspoon garlic powder
- Salt and pepper to taste
- 1 cup cooked brown rice
- Lemon wedges for serving

Instructions:

1. Preheat the grill to medium-high heat. Brush the tilapia fillets with olive oil and season with paprika, garlic powder, salt, and pepper.
2. Grill the tilapia for 3-4 minutes per side until the fish is cooked through and flakes easily.
3. Serve the grilled tilapia over a bed of brown rice with lemon wedges on the side.

Spaghetti Squash with Marinara Sauce

Ingredients:

- 1 medium spaghetti squash
- 2 cups marinara sauce
- 1 tablespoon olive oil
- Salt and pepper to taste
- Fresh basil, chopped (optional)
- Grated Parmesan cheese (optional)

Instructions:

1. Preheat the oven to 400°F (200°C). Cut the spaghetti squash in half lengthwise and scoop out the seeds.
2. Drizzle olive oil over the squash halves and season with salt and pepper. Place cut side down on a baking sheet.
3. Roast for 40-45 minutes until the squash is tender and easily shreds into spaghetti-like strands with a fork.
4. Heat marinara sauce in a pan over medium heat. Once the squash is done, shred the flesh with a fork and top with marinara sauce.
5. Garnish with fresh basil and grated Parmesan, if desired. Serve immediately.

Baked Cod with Asparagus

Ingredients:

- 2 cod fillets
- 1 bunch asparagus, trimmed
- 2 tablespoons olive oil
- 1 teaspoon lemon zest
- 1 tablespoon lemon juice
- Salt and pepper to taste

Instructions:

1. Preheat the oven to 400°F (200°C). Place the cod fillets on a baking sheet and drizzle with 1 tablespoon olive oil, lemon zest, salt, and pepper.
2. Arrange the asparagus around the fish, drizzle with the remaining olive oil, and season with salt and pepper.
3. Bake for 12-15 minutes until the fish is cooked through and flakes easily with a fork, and the asparagus is tender.
4. Serve the cod and asparagus with a squeeze of fresh lemon juice.

Cauliflower Rice Stir-Fry

Ingredients:

- 1 medium cauliflower, grated into rice-sized pieces (or use pre-made cauliflower rice)
- 1 tablespoon olive oil
- 1/2 onion, chopped
- 1/2 cup bell pepper, diced
- 1/2 cup carrots, julienned
- 1/4 cup peas
- 2 garlic cloves, minced
- 2 tablespoons soy sauce or tamari (for gluten-free)
- 1 teaspoon sesame oil (optional)
- 1/4 teaspoon ground ginger
- Salt and pepper to taste

Instructions:

1. Heat olive oil in a large skillet or wok over medium heat. Add onion, bell pepper, and carrots. Sauté for 4-5 minutes until softened.
2. Add peas and garlic, cooking for another minute.
3. Stir in cauliflower rice, soy sauce, sesame oil, ginger, salt, and pepper. Cook for 5-7 minutes, stirring occasionally, until the cauliflower rice is tender.
4. Serve warm as a side dish or light meal.

Chicken and Vegetable Skewers

Ingredients:

- 2 boneless, skinless chicken breasts, cut into cubes
- 1 zucchini, sliced
- 1 red bell pepper, cut into chunks
- 1/2 onion, cut into chunks
- 1 tablespoon olive oil
- 1 tablespoon lemon juice
- 1 teaspoon dried oregano
- Salt and pepper to taste
- Wooden skewers (soaked in water for 30 minutes)

Instructions:

1. Preheat the grill to medium-high heat. In a bowl, mix olive oil, lemon juice, oregano, salt, and pepper.
2. Thread chicken, zucchini, bell pepper, and onion onto skewers.
3. Brush the skewers with the marinade and grill for 10-12 minutes, turning occasionally, until the chicken is cooked through and the vegetables are tender.
4. Serve immediately with a side of quinoa or rice.

Baked Turkey Meatballs with Zoodles

Ingredients for Meatballs:

- 1 lb ground turkey
- 1/4 cup breadcrumbs
- 1 egg
- 1/4 cup Parmesan cheese, grated
- 2 garlic cloves, minced
- 1 teaspoon dried oregano
- Salt and pepper to taste

For Zoodles:

- 2 medium zucchinis, spiralized into noodles
- 1 tablespoon olive oil
- 1/2 cup marinara sauce

Instructions:

1. Preheat the oven to 375°F (190°C). In a bowl, combine ground turkey, breadcrumbs, egg, Parmesan, garlic, oregano, salt, and pepper.
2. Form the mixture into small meatballs and place on a baking sheet.
3. Bake for 20-25 minutes until cooked through and golden.
4. While the meatballs bake, heat olive oil in a skillet and sauté the zucchini noodles for 3-4 minutes until tender.
5. Serve the meatballs on top of the zoodles with marinara sauce.

Lentil and Vegetable Soup

Ingredients:

- 1 cup dried lentils, rinsed
- 1 tablespoon olive oil
- 1 onion, chopped
- 2 carrots, chopped
- 2 celery stalks, chopped
- 2 garlic cloves, minced
- 1 zucchini, chopped
- 1 can (14.5 oz) diced tomatoes
- 4 cups vegetable broth
- 1 teaspoon dried thyme
- 1/2 teaspoon ground cumin
- Salt and pepper to taste
- Fresh parsley for garnish

Instructions:

1. Heat olive oil in a large pot over medium heat. Add onion, carrots, and celery, cooking until softened, about 5-7 minutes.
2. Add garlic and zucchini, cooking for 1 minute.
3. Stir in lentils, diced tomatoes, vegetable broth, thyme, cumin, salt, and pepper.
4. Bring to a boil, then reduce heat and simmer for 30-35 minutes until the lentils are tender.
5. Garnish with fresh parsley and serve warm.

Spicy Baked Tofu with Steamed Greens

Ingredients:

- 1 block firm tofu, pressed and cut into cubes
- 2 tablespoons soy sauce
- 1 tablespoon sriracha sauce
- 1 tablespoon sesame oil
- 1 teaspoon garlic powder
- Salt to taste
- 2 cups greens (spinach, kale, or bok choy), steamed

Instructions:

1. Preheat the oven to 375°F (190°C). In a bowl, combine soy sauce, sriracha, sesame oil, garlic powder, and salt.
2. Toss tofu cubes in the sauce mixture and place them on a baking sheet.
3. Bake for 25-30 minutes, flipping halfway through, until crispy and golden.
4. Steam your choice of greens for 4-5 minutes until tender.
5. Serve the spicy tofu over the steamed greens and enjoy.

Stuffed Bell Peppers with Ground Turkey

Ingredients:

- 4 bell peppers, tops cut off and seeds removed
- 1 lb ground turkey
- 1/2 cup cooked quinoa or rice
- 1/2 cup diced tomatoes
- 1 teaspoon garlic powder
- 1 teaspoon dried oregano
- Salt and pepper to taste
- 1/2 cup shredded mozzarella cheese

Instructions:

1. Preheat the oven to 375°F (190°C). In a skillet, cook ground turkey over medium heat until browned.
2. Stir in cooked quinoa or rice, diced tomatoes, garlic powder, oregano, salt, and pepper. Cook for 2-3 minutes until well combined.
3. Stuff the bell peppers with the turkey mixture and place them in a baking dish.
4. Sprinkle with mozzarella cheese and bake for 20-25 minutes, until the peppers are tender and the cheese is melted.
5. Serve warm.

Grilled Chicken Caesar Salad (light dressing)

Ingredients for Salad:

- 2 boneless, skinless chicken breasts
- 4 cups Romaine lettuce, chopped
- 1/4 cup grated Parmesan cheese
- Croutons (optional)

For Light Caesar Dressing:

- 1/4 cup Greek yogurt
- 2 tablespoons lemon juice
- 1 tablespoon Dijon mustard
- 1 tablespoon olive oil
- 1/2 teaspoon garlic powder
- Salt and pepper to taste

Instructions:

1. Preheat the grill to medium-high heat. Season the chicken breasts with olive oil, salt, and pepper.
2. Grill the chicken for 6-8 minutes per side, until the internal temperature reaches 165°F (74°C).
3. While the chicken cooks, mix all the ingredients for the light Caesar dressing in a small bowl.
4. Slice the grilled chicken and toss it with chopped lettuce, Parmesan, and croutons.
5. Drizzle with the dressing and serve immediately.

Black Bean and Quinoa Salad

Ingredients:

- 1 cup cooked quinoa
- 1 can (15 oz) black beans, drained and rinsed
- 1 cup corn kernels (fresh or frozen)
- 1 red bell pepper, diced
- 1/4 cup red onion, finely chopped
- 1/4 cup cilantro, chopped
- Juice of 1 lime
- 2 tablespoons olive oil
- Salt and pepper to taste

Instructions:

1. In a large bowl, combine quinoa, black beans, corn, bell pepper, red onion, and cilantro.
2. Drizzle with lime juice, olive oil, salt, and pepper. Toss to combine.
3. Serve chilled or at room temperature.

Salmon with Roasted Brussels Sprouts

Ingredients:

- 2 salmon fillets
- 1 lb Brussels sprouts, trimmed and halved
- 1 tablespoon olive oil
- Salt and pepper to taste
- 1 tablespoon lemon juice

Instructions:

1. Preheat the oven to 400°F (200°C). Place the Brussels sprouts on a baking sheet and drizzle with olive oil, salt, and pepper. Toss to coat.
2. Roast for 20 minutes, flipping halfway through.
3. Season the salmon fillets with salt and pepper and place them on a separate baking sheet.
4. Roast the salmon for 12-15 minutes, or until the internal temperature reaches 145°F (63°C).
5. Serve the roasted Brussels sprouts with the salmon and drizzle with lemon juice.

Chicken Lettuce Wraps

Ingredients:

- 1 lb ground chicken
- 1 tablespoon olive oil
- 1/2 onion, chopped
- 2 garlic cloves, minced
- 1/4 cup soy sauce
- 1 tablespoon hoisin sauce
- 1 tablespoon rice vinegar
- 1/4 cup water chestnuts, chopped
- 1/4 cup green onions, chopped
- 1 head Romaine lettuce, leaves separated

Instructions:

1. Heat olive oil in a skillet over medium heat. Add the ground chicken and cook until browned.
2. Stir in onion, garlic, soy sauce, hoisin sauce, and rice vinegar. Cook for 2-3 minutes until the mixture is well combined.
3. Add water chestnuts and green onions, cooking for an additional 1-2 minutes.
4. Spoon the chicken mixture into individual Romaine lettuce leaves and serve.

Veggie and Chickpea Curry

Ingredients:

- 1 tablespoon olive oil
- 1 onion, chopped
- 2 garlic cloves, minced
- 1 tablespoon ginger, grated
- 1 can (15 oz) chickpeas, drained and rinsed
- 1 zucchini, chopped
- 1 red bell pepper, chopped
- 1 can (14.5 oz) diced tomatoes
- 1 can (14 oz) coconut milk
- 2 tablespoons curry powder
- Salt and pepper to taste
- Fresh cilantro for garnish

Instructions:

1. Heat olive oil in a large pan over medium heat. Add onion, garlic, and ginger and sauté for 3-4 minutes.
2. Stir in chickpeas, zucchini, red bell pepper, diced tomatoes, coconut milk, curry powder, salt, and pepper.
3. Simmer for 15-20 minutes until the vegetables are tender and the curry is thickened.
4. Garnish with fresh cilantro and serve with rice or naan bread.

Baked Chicken Parmesan with Zucchini Noodles

Ingredients:

- 2 boneless, skinless chicken breasts
- 1 cup breadcrumbs
- 1/2 cup grated Parmesan cheese
- 1 egg, beaten
- 1 cup marinara sauce
- 1/2 cup shredded mozzarella cheese
- 3 medium zucchinis, spiralized into noodles
- 1 tablespoon olive oil
- Salt and pepper to taste

Instructions:

1. Preheat the oven to 375°F (190°C). Season chicken breasts with salt and pepper, then dip in beaten egg and coat with breadcrumbs mixed with Parmesan cheese.
2. Place the chicken on a baking sheet and bake for 20-25 minutes until cooked through.
3. In a skillet, heat olive oil over medium heat and sauté zucchini noodles for 2-3 minutes until tender.
4. Top each baked chicken breast with marinara sauce and mozzarella cheese, then return to the oven for 5-7 minutes until the cheese is melted and bubbly.
5. Serve the chicken Parmesan over the zucchini noodles.

Grilled Veggie Skewers

Ingredients:

- 1 red bell pepper, cut into chunks
- 1 zucchini, sliced
- 1 red onion, cut into chunks
- 8-10 cherry tomatoes
- 1 tablespoon olive oil
- 1 teaspoon dried oregano
- Salt and pepper to taste
- Wooden skewers (soaked in water for 30 minutes)

Instructions:

1. Preheat the grill to medium-high heat.
2. Thread vegetables onto the skewers, alternating between bell pepper, zucchini, onion, and cherry tomatoes.
3. Drizzle the skewers with olive oil, and season with oregano, salt, and pepper.
4. Grill the skewers for 5-7 minutes, turning occasionally, until the vegetables are tender and lightly charred.
5. Serve warm as a side dish.

Eggplant Stir-Fry with Tofu

Ingredients:

- 1 block firm tofu, pressed and cubed
- 1 eggplant, chopped
- 1 red bell pepper, sliced
- 1 tablespoon olive oil
- 2 tablespoons soy sauce
- 1 tablespoon hoisin sauce
- 1 teaspoon garlic powder
- 1 teaspoon sesame oil
- Fresh cilantro for garnish

Instructions:

1. Heat olive oil in a large skillet or wok over medium heat. Add tofu and cook until golden brown on all sides. Remove and set aside.
2. In the same skillet, add eggplant and bell pepper. Sauté for 5-7 minutes until tender.
3. Add soy sauce, hoisin sauce, garlic powder, and sesame oil. Stir to combine.
4. Return the tofu to the skillet and cook for another 2-3 minutes, allowing the flavors to combine.
5. Garnish with fresh cilantro and serve immediately.

Shrimp and Avocado Salad

Ingredients:

- 1 lb cooked shrimp, peeled and deveined
- 2 ripe avocados, diced
- 1 cup cherry tomatoes, halved
- 1/2 red onion, thinly sliced
- 1 tablespoon olive oil
- 1 tablespoon lime juice
- 1 tablespoon fresh cilantro, chopped
- Salt and pepper to taste

Instructions:

1. In a large bowl, combine shrimp, avocado, cherry tomatoes, and red onion.
2. Drizzle with olive oil and lime juice. Toss gently to combine.
3. Season with salt, pepper, and fresh cilantro.
4. Serve immediately as a refreshing salad.

Roasted Sweet Potato with Black Beans

Ingredients:

- 2 large sweet potatoes, peeled and cubed
- 1 can (15 oz) black beans, drained and rinsed
- 1 tablespoon olive oil
- 1 teaspoon chili powder
- 1/2 teaspoon cumin
- Salt and pepper to taste
- Fresh cilantro for garnish
- Lime wedges for serving

Instructions:

1. Preheat the oven to 400°F (200°C). Toss sweet potato cubes with olive oil, chili powder, cumin, salt, and pepper.
2. Spread the sweet potatoes on a baking sheet and roast for 25-30 minutes, flipping halfway through.
3. In the last 5 minutes of roasting, add black beans to the baking sheet to warm them.
4. Serve the roasted sweet potatoes and black beans garnished with fresh cilantro and lime wedges.

Chicken Fajitas with Bell Peppers

Ingredients:

- 2 boneless, skinless chicken breasts, sliced into strips
- 1 red bell pepper, sliced
- 1 yellow bell pepper, sliced
- 1 onion, sliced
- 2 tablespoons olive oil
- 1 tablespoon lime juice
- 1 teaspoon chili powder
- 1/2 teaspoon cumin
- Salt and pepper to taste
- Flour tortillas for serving

Instructions:

1. Heat olive oil in a skillet over medium heat. Add chicken strips and cook for 5-7 minutes until browned and cooked through.
2. Add bell peppers and onion to the skillet. Cook for an additional 5 minutes until the vegetables are tender.
3. Stir in lime juice, chili powder, cumin, salt, and pepper.
4. Serve the fajita mixture in warm flour tortillas.

Roasted Salmon with Cucumber and Tomato Salad

Ingredients for Salmon:

- 2 salmon fillets
- 1 tablespoon olive oil
- 1 teaspoon garlic powder
- Salt and pepper to taste

For Salad:

- 1 cucumber, sliced
- 1 cup cherry tomatoes, halved
- 1 tablespoon red onion, finely chopped
- 1 tablespoon fresh dill, chopped
- 1 tablespoon olive oil
- 1 tablespoon lemon juice
- Salt and pepper to taste

Instructions:

1. Preheat the oven to 375°F (190°C). Place the salmon fillets on a baking sheet, drizzle with olive oil, and season with garlic powder, salt, and pepper.
2. Roast for 12-15 minutes until the salmon is cooked through and flakes easily with a fork.
3. While the salmon bakes, prepare the salad by mixing cucumber, tomatoes, red onion, dill, olive oil, lemon juice, salt, and pepper in a bowl.
4. Serve the roasted salmon alongside the cucumber and tomato salad.

Lemon Garlic Grilled Shrimp

Ingredients:

- 1 lb shrimp, peeled and deveined
- 2 tablespoons olive oil
- 2 garlic cloves, minced
- Juice of 1 lemon
- 1 teaspoon paprika
- Salt and pepper to taste

Instructions:

1. In a bowl, mix olive oil, garlic, lemon juice, paprika, salt, and pepper.
2. Toss shrimp in the marinade and let sit for 10-15 minutes.
3. Preheat the grill to medium-high heat and grill shrimp for 2-3 minutes per side until cooked through.
4. Serve with extra lemon wedges and enjoy!

Chickpea and Spinach Stew

Ingredients:

- 1 can (15 oz) chickpeas, drained and rinsed
- 4 cups fresh spinach
- 1 tablespoon olive oil
- 1 onion, chopped
- 2 garlic cloves, minced
- 1 teaspoon ground cumin
- 1/2 teaspoon paprika
- 1 can (14.5 oz) diced tomatoes
- 2 cups vegetable broth
- Salt and pepper to taste

Instructions:

1. Heat olive oil in a pot over medium heat. Add onion and cook for 4-5 minutes until softened.
2. Add garlic, cumin, and paprika and cook for 1 minute.
3. Stir in chickpeas, diced tomatoes, and vegetable broth. Bring to a boil, then reduce heat and simmer for 10 minutes.
4. Add spinach and cook for another 2-3 minutes until wilted.
5. Season with salt and pepper, then serve warm.

Roasted Cauliflower with Tahini Dressing

Ingredients:

- 1 head cauliflower, cut into florets
- 2 tablespoons olive oil
- Salt and pepper to taste
- 1/4 cup tahini
- 1 tablespoon lemon juice
- 1 tablespoon water (for thinning)
- 1 teaspoon garlic powder

Instructions:

1. Preheat the oven to 400°F (200°C). Toss cauliflower florets with olive oil, salt, and pepper.
2. Roast for 25-30 minutes, flipping halfway through, until golden and tender.
3. In a small bowl, whisk together tahini, lemon juice, water, and garlic powder to make the dressing.
4. Drizzle the tahini dressing over the roasted cauliflower and serve warm.

Grilled Portobello Mushrooms with Quinoa

Ingredients:

- 4 large Portobello mushroom caps
- 2 tablespoons olive oil
- 1 teaspoon balsamic vinegar
- 1 cup cooked quinoa
- 1/4 cup fresh parsley, chopped
- Salt and pepper to taste

Instructions:

1. Preheat the grill to medium-high heat. Brush mushroom caps with olive oil and balsamic vinegar, and season with salt and pepper.
2. Grill the mushrooms for 5-7 minutes per side until tender.
3. While the mushrooms cook, prepare the quinoa and stir in fresh parsley.
4. Serve the grilled mushrooms over quinoa for a hearty meal.

Sautéed Spinach and Garlic Chicken

Ingredients:

- 2 boneless, skinless chicken breasts
- 1 tablespoon olive oil
- 3 garlic cloves, minced
- 4 cups fresh spinach
- 1/4 teaspoon red pepper flakes (optional)
- Salt and pepper to taste
- 1 tablespoon lemon juice

Instructions:

1. Heat olive oil in a skillet over medium heat. Season chicken breasts with salt and pepper.
2. Cook the chicken for 6-7 minutes per side until golden brown and cooked through (internal temperature should reach 165°F or 74°C). Remove and set aside.
3. In the same skillet, add garlic and sauté for 1-2 minutes until fragrant.
4. Add spinach and red pepper flakes (if using), cooking for 2-3 minutes until wilted.
5. Stir in lemon juice and serve the chicken on top of the sautéed spinach.

Veggie-Packed Whole Wheat Pasta

Ingredients:

- 8 oz whole wheat pasta
- 1 tablespoon olive oil
- 1/2 cup cherry tomatoes, halved
- 1 zucchini, diced
- 1 bell pepper, diced
- 1/2 onion, chopped
- 2 garlic cloves, minced
- 1/4 teaspoon dried basil
- Salt and pepper to taste
- Fresh Parmesan cheese for garnish (optional)

Instructions:

1. Cook whole wheat pasta according to package instructions. Drain and set aside.
2. In a large skillet, heat olive oil over medium heat. Add onions, bell pepper, zucchini, and cherry tomatoes. Sauté for 5-7 minutes until the vegetables are tender.
3. Add garlic, basil, salt, and pepper, cooking for another 1-2 minutes.
4. Toss the cooked pasta with the vegetables and serve with a sprinkle of Parmesan cheese if desired.

Grilled Chicken and Cucumber Salad

Ingredients:

- 2 boneless, skinless chicken breasts
- 1 tablespoon olive oil
- 1 teaspoon dried oregano
- 1/2 teaspoon garlic powder
- Salt and pepper to taste
- 2 cucumbers, thinly sliced
- 1/2 red onion, thinly sliced
- 1/4 cup fresh parsley, chopped
- 1 tablespoon red wine vinegar

Instructions:

1. Preheat the grill to medium-high heat. Brush chicken breasts with olive oil and season with oregano, garlic powder, salt, and pepper.
2. Grill the chicken for 6-7 minutes per side until cooked through (internal temperature should reach 165°F or 74°C).
3. While the chicken cooks, combine cucumber, onion, parsley, and red wine vinegar in a bowl. Season with salt and pepper.
4. Slice the grilled chicken and serve on top of the cucumber salad.

Spicy Grilled Shrimp with Avocado Salsa

Ingredients:

- 1 lb shrimp, peeled and deveined
- 1 tablespoon olive oil
- 1 tablespoon chili powder
- 1/2 teaspoon cayenne pepper
- Salt and pepper to taste
- 1 avocado, diced
- 1/2 red onion, diced
- 1/2 cup cilantro, chopped
- 1 tablespoon lime juice

Instructions:

1. Preheat the grill to medium-high heat. Toss shrimp with olive oil, chili powder, cayenne pepper, salt, and pepper.
2. Grill shrimp for 2-3 minutes per side until pink and cooked through.
3. In a bowl, combine avocado, onion, cilantro, and lime juice. Season with salt and pepper.
4. Serve the grilled shrimp with the avocado salsa on top.

Quinoa-Stuffed Tomatoes

Ingredients:

- 4 large tomatoes
- 1 cup cooked quinoa
- 1/4 cup fresh basil, chopped
- 1/4 cup feta cheese, crumbled
- 1 tablespoon olive oil
- Salt and pepper to taste

Instructions:

1. Preheat the oven to 375°F (190°C). Cut the tops off the tomatoes and scoop out the insides, discarding the seeds and pulp.
2. In a bowl, mix cooked quinoa, basil, feta cheese, olive oil, salt, and pepper.
3. Stuff the tomatoes with the quinoa mixture and place them in a baking dish.
4. Bake for 20-25 minutes until the tomatoes are tender. Serve warm.

Light Turkey Chili

Ingredients:

- 1 lb ground turkey
- 1 tablespoon olive oil
- 1 onion, chopped
- 1 bell pepper, chopped
- 2 garlic cloves, minced
- 1 can (15 oz) diced tomatoes
- 1 can (15 oz) kidney beans, drained and rinsed
- 1 can (15 oz) black beans, drained and rinsed
- 1 tablespoon chili powder
- 1/2 teaspoon cumin
- Salt and pepper to taste

Instructions:

1. In a large pot, heat olive oil over medium heat. Add ground turkey and cook until browned, breaking it apart as it cooks.
2. Add onion, bell pepper, and garlic, cooking for 5-7 minutes until softened.
3. Stir in diced tomatoes, beans, chili powder, cumin, salt, and pepper. Bring to a simmer.
4. Cook for 20-25 minutes, stirring occasionally, until the flavors have melded together. Serve warm.

Grilled Eggplant and Tomato Stack

Ingredients:

- 2 medium eggplants, sliced into rounds
- 2 tomatoes, sliced
- 1/4 cup fresh basil, chopped
- 1 tablespoon olive oil
- 1 teaspoon balsamic vinegar
- Salt and pepper to taste

Instructions:

1. Preheat the grill to medium-high heat. Brush eggplant slices with olive oil and season with salt and pepper.
2. Grill the eggplant for 3-4 minutes per side until tender and slightly charred.
3. Stack grilled eggplant slices with tomato slices and fresh basil.
4. Drizzle with balsamic vinegar and serve immediately.

Spaghetti Squash with Garlic and Herbs

Ingredients:

- 1 medium spaghetti squash
- 2 tablespoons olive oil
- 2 garlic cloves, minced
- 1 tablespoon fresh parsley, chopped
- 1/2 teaspoon dried thyme
- Salt and pepper to taste

Instructions:

1. Preheat the oven to 400°F (200°C). Slice the spaghetti squash in half lengthwise and remove the seeds.
2. Drizzle the inside of the squash with olive oil, season with salt and pepper, and place it cut-side down on a baking sheet.
3. Roast for 40-45 minutes until tender. Use a fork to scrape out the strands of squash.
4. In a skillet, heat olive oil and sauté garlic for 1-2 minutes until fragrant.
5. Toss the spaghetti squash with garlic, parsley, thyme, salt, and pepper. Serve warm.

Shrimp Scampi with Zucchini Noodles

Ingredients:

- 1 lb shrimp, peeled and deveined
- 2 tablespoons olive oil
- 2 garlic cloves, minced
- 1/4 cup white wine (or chicken broth)
- 2 tablespoons lemon juice
- 1/4 teaspoon red pepper flakes
- 4 medium zucchinis, spiralized into noodles
- Salt and pepper to taste
- Fresh parsley for garnish

Instructions:

1. Heat olive oil in a large skillet over medium heat. Add shrimp and cook for 2-3 minutes per side until pink and cooked through. Remove and set aside.
2. In the same skillet, add garlic and cook for 1 minute until fragrant.
3. Stir in white wine, lemon juice, and red pepper flakes. Cook for another 2 minutes.
4. Add zucchini noodles to the skillet and cook for 2-3 minutes until tender.
5. Add shrimp back into the skillet and toss everything together. Season with salt and pepper.
6. Garnish with fresh parsley and serve immediately.

Grilled Turkey Burgers with Sweet Potato Fries

Ingredients for Turkey Burgers:

- 1 lb ground turkey
- 1/4 cup breadcrumbs
- 1/4 cup grated Parmesan cheese
- 1 tablespoon fresh parsley, chopped
- 1 teaspoon garlic powder
- Salt and pepper to taste

For Sweet Potato Fries:

- 2 medium sweet potatoes, peeled and cut into fries
- 1 tablespoon olive oil
- 1 teaspoon paprika
- Salt and pepper to taste

Instructions:

1. Preheat the grill to medium-high heat. In a bowl, combine ground turkey, breadcrumbs, Parmesan, parsley, garlic powder, salt, and pepper. Form into patties.
2. Grill turkey burgers for 5-7 minutes per side until cooked through (internal temperature should reach 165°F or 74°C).
3. Preheat the oven to 400°F (200°C). Toss sweet potato fries with olive oil, paprika, salt, and pepper.
4. Spread the fries on a baking sheet and roast for 20-25 minutes, flipping halfway through, until crispy and tender.
5. Serve the turkey burgers with sweet potato fries on the side.

Quinoa and Black Bean Lettuce Wraps

Ingredients:

- 1 cup cooked quinoa
- 1 can (15 oz) black beans, drained and rinsed
- 1/2 red bell pepper, diced
- 1/4 cup corn kernels (fresh or frozen)
- 1/4 cup fresh cilantro, chopped
- 1 tablespoon lime juice
- Salt and pepper to taste
- 12 large lettuce leaves (such as Romaine or Butter lettuce)

Instructions:

1. In a bowl, combine cooked quinoa, black beans, red bell pepper, corn, cilantro, lime juice, salt, and pepper.
2. Gently separate the lettuce leaves and wash them thoroughly.
3. Spoon the quinoa mixture into the center of each lettuce leaf and serve as a wrap.

Roasted Veggie Buddha Bowl

Ingredients:

- 1 cup cooked quinoa or brown rice
- 1 sweet potato, peeled and cubed
- 1 cup broccoli florets
- 1/2 cup chickpeas, drained and rinsed
- 1 tablespoon olive oil
- 1 teaspoon paprika
- Salt and pepper to taste
- 1/4 cup tahini dressing (store-bought or homemade)

Instructions:

1. Preheat the oven to 400°F (200°C). On a baking sheet, toss sweet potato, broccoli, and chickpeas with olive oil, paprika, salt, and pepper.
2. Roast for 20-25 minutes, flipping halfway through, until vegetables are tender.
3. Assemble the bowl by layering quinoa or rice, roasted vegetables, and chickpeas.
4. Drizzle with tahini dressing and serve warm.

Baked Chicken with Roasted Veggies

Ingredients:

- 2 boneless, skinless chicken breasts
- 1 tablespoon olive oil
- 1 teaspoon garlic powder
- 1 teaspoon dried rosemary
- Salt and pepper to taste
- 1 cup baby carrots
- 1 cup Brussels sprouts, halved
- 1 tablespoon olive oil (for veggies)

Instructions:

1. Preheat the oven to 375°F (190°C). Place chicken breasts on a baking sheet and drizzle with olive oil. Sprinkle with garlic powder, rosemary, salt, and pepper.
2. On another baking sheet, toss carrots and Brussels sprouts with olive oil, salt, and pepper.
3. Bake the chicken for 25-30 minutes until cooked through (internal temperature should reach 165°F or 74°C) and roast the vegetables for 20-25 minutes until tender.
4. Serve the chicken with the roasted vegetables on the side.

Tofu Stir-Fry with Brown Rice

Ingredients:

- 1 block firm tofu, pressed and cubed
- 2 tablespoons soy sauce
- 1 tablespoon sesame oil
- 1 tablespoon olive oil
- 1 red bell pepper, sliced
- 1 carrot, julienned
- 1/2 cup snow peas
- 1/4 cup green onions, chopped
- 2 cups cooked brown rice
- 1 teaspoon sesame seeds (optional)

Instructions:

1. In a bowl, toss tofu cubes with soy sauce and sesame oil. Let marinate for 10 minutes.
2. Heat olive oil in a large skillet or wok over medium-high heat. Add tofu and cook for 5-7 minutes until golden and crispy on all sides. Remove and set aside.
3. In the same skillet, add red bell pepper, carrot, snow peas, and green onions. Sauté for 3-4 minutes until vegetables are tender-crisp.
4. Add cooked brown rice and tofu back to the skillet. Toss to combine and heat through.
5. Garnish with sesame seeds and serve warm.

Spaghetti with Tomato Basil Sauce

Ingredients:

- 8 oz whole wheat spaghetti
- 1 can (15 oz) crushed tomatoes
- 2 tablespoons olive oil
- 2 garlic cloves, minced
- 1/4 teaspoon red pepper flakes (optional)
- 1/4 cup fresh basil, chopped
- Salt and pepper to taste
- Fresh Parmesan cheese for garnish (optional)

Instructions:

1. Cook the spaghetti according to package instructions. Drain and set aside.
2. In a skillet, heat olive oil over medium heat. Add garlic and red pepper flakes (if using), sautéing for 1-2 minutes until fragrant.
3. Stir in crushed tomatoes and cook for 10 minutes, allowing the sauce to thicken.
4. Add fresh basil, salt, and pepper. Toss the spaghetti with the tomato sauce.
5. Garnish with Parmesan cheese and serve warm.

Grilled Chicken with Mango Salsa

Ingredients:

- 2 boneless, skinless chicken breasts
- 1 tablespoon olive oil
- Salt and pepper to taste
- 1 mango, diced
- 1/4 red onion, diced
- 1/4 cup fresh cilantro, chopped
- Juice of 1 lime

Instructions:

1. Preheat the grill to medium-high heat. Brush chicken breasts with olive oil and season with salt and pepper.
2. Grill the chicken for 6-7 minutes per side until fully cooked (internal temperature should reach 165°F or 74°C).
3. In a bowl, combine diced mango, red onion, cilantro, and lime juice to make the salsa.
4. Serve the grilled chicken topped with fresh mango salsa.

Sweet Potato and Kale Salad

Ingredients:

- 2 medium sweet potatoes, peeled and cubed
- 2 tablespoons olive oil
- Salt and pepper to taste
- 4 cups fresh kale, chopped
- 1/4 cup toasted pumpkin seeds
- 1/4 cup dried cranberries
- 1 tablespoon balsamic vinegar

Instructions:

1. Preheat the oven to 400°F (200°C). Toss sweet potato cubes with olive oil, salt, and pepper. Roast for 20-25 minutes until tender and golden.
2. While the sweet potatoes roast, massage the kale with a little olive oil and a pinch of salt to soften the leaves.
3. Once the sweet potatoes are done, combine them with the kale, toasted pumpkin seeds, and dried cranberries.
4. Drizzle with balsamic vinegar and toss. Serve warm or at room temperature.

Grilled Shrimp Tacos with Slaw

Ingredients for Shrimp:

- 1 lb shrimp, peeled and deveined
- 1 tablespoon olive oil
- 1 teaspoon chili powder
- 1 teaspoon cumin
- Salt and pepper to taste
- Juice of 1 lime

For Slaw:

- 2 cups shredded cabbage
- 1/4 cup Greek yogurt
- 1 tablespoon lime juice
- 1 teaspoon honey
- Salt and pepper to taste

For Tacos:

- 8 small corn tortillas
- Fresh cilantro for garnish

Instructions:

1. Preheat the grill to medium-high heat. Toss shrimp with olive oil, chili powder, cumin, salt, and pepper.
2. Grill shrimp for 2-3 minutes per side until pink and cooked through. Drizzle with lime juice.
3. In a bowl, combine shredded cabbage, Greek yogurt, lime juice, honey, salt, and pepper to make the slaw.
4. Warm the corn tortillas on the grill for 1-2 minutes.
5. Assemble tacos by placing shrimp on the tortillas and topping with slaw and fresh cilantro. Serve immediately.

www.ingramcontent.com/pod-product-compliance
Lightning Source LLC
LaVergne TN
LVHW081341060526
838201LV00055B/2784